A NATION'S FIRST STEPS

Douglas Baldwin

Weigl

CALGARY

www.weigl.com

We acknowledge the financial support of the Government of Canada through the Book Publishing Industry Development Program (BPIDP) for our publishing activities.

Published by Weigl Educational Publishers Limited
6325 – 10 Street SE
Calgary, Alberta, Canada
T2H 2Z9

Web site: www.weigl.com

National Library of Canada Cataloguing-in-Publication Data

Baldwin, Douglas, 1944-
    A nation's first steps / Douglas Baldwin.

(Canadian history)
Includes bibliographical references and index.
For use in grades 6-8.
ISBN 1-55388-015-3

    1. Canada--History--1867- --Juvenile literature. I. Title. II. Series: Canadian history (Calgary, Alta.)

FC3206.B34 2002   971.05   C2002-901448-4
F1060.9.B343 2002

Printed in the United States of America
1 2 3 4 5 6 7 8 9 0   06 05 04 03 02

Project Coordinator
Michael Lowry
Editor
Lynn Hamilton
Copy Editor
Nicole Bezic King
Photo Researcher
Gayle Murdoff
Designer
Warren Clark
Layout
Terry Paulhus

CONTENTS

Union and EXPANSION

Although Canada was one of the largest countries in the world, its population was less than 4 million.

In 1864, the Province of Canada urged the Atlantic colonies to unite with them to form a new nation. They were reluctant. In New Brunswick and Nova Scotia, merchants feared competition from Canada. People from Prince Edward Island wondered how their interests could be protected by only six representatives in Ottawa. Newfoundlanders worried that their trade with Britain and the United States would suffer. However, fears of American invasion and the desire for a transcontinental railway prompted New Brunswick and Nova Scotia to reconsider. On July 1, 1867, New Brunswick, Nova Scotia, and the Province of Canada united to form the Dominion of Canada. Canada's first prime minister was Sir John A. Macdonald.

In 1869, Canada purchased Rupert's Land from the Hudson's Bay Company. Threatened by the potential settlement of **Métis** territory, Louis Riel fought to defend his people's land rights. Following confrontations between Métis and Canadian supporters, Macdonald agreed to Métis demands. The small tract of land around the Red River settlement became Manitoba in 1870. The rest of Rupert's Land was named the North-West Territories.

British Columbia entered Confederation in 1871, after it was promised **responsible government**, help with its debt, a public-works program, and a railway. Canada also made promises to Prince Edward Island, which included covering its debts and solving difficulties with **absentee landlords**. PEI joined in 1873.

The Dream

Although Canada was one of the largest countries in the world in terms of land size,

■ On June 29, 1927, a stamp of the Ottawa Parliament buildings was issued to commemorate the sixtieth anniversary of Confederation.

its population was less than 4 million. Its economy was based upon natural resources, such as fertile land, timber, and fish. To increase Canada's population and to promote industrial growth, Macdonald adopted the National Policy.

The main feature of the National Policy was protective tariffs. These taxes meant that manufactured goods from other countries would cost more than Canadian-made goods. Macdonald believed these tariffs would allow Canadian businesses to compete with American and British firms.

Macdonald also encouraged people from the United States, Britain, and Europe to settle in Canada, especially in the West. He set up a homesteading policy called the Dominion Lands Act.

Finally, Macdonald wanted a railway to unite the country from sea to sea. This railway would carry settlers to the West and could transport soldiers if the need arose. Freight cars would take the agricultural goods of the West to eastern markets and return with the East's manufactured goods. Before a railway could be built and people could move West, the government would have to reach an agreement with the Aboriginal peoples and the Métis.

SIR JOHN A. MACDONALD

John A. Macdonald was born in Scotland in 1815 and moved to Canada with his family when he was 5 years old. He spent several years studying and practising law. In 1844, he won a **Conservative** seat in the Assembly of the Province of Canada. He would eventually serve two terms as prime minister, the first from 1867 to 1873. Macdonald was strongly committed to the union of the colonies and played a key role in negotiations leading to Confederation in 1867. As a result, he is considered one of the "Fathers of Confederation."

After Confederation, Macdonald focused on expansion of the West. Under his leadership, the Manitoba Act of 1870 was passed, adding a fifth province to the Dominion of Canada. In 1871, British Columbia was persuaded to join, followed by Prince Edward Island in 1873. Despite political controversies, Macdonald was instrumental in the development of a transcontinental railway. However, a scandal over the railway led to his resignation in 1873. He became prime minister again in 1878, as a result of his policy on tariffs. He held the position until his death in 1891.

■ John A. Macdonald was a lawyer before he became a politician.

DISASTER for a Traditional Way of Life

At first, the Aboriginal peoples profited from the fur trade without losing their traditional way of life. For many, the fur trade provided them with new items that improved their lifestyle, such as metal axes, guns, cloth, and sewing needles. However, the nineteenth century was a century of great change, and the 1870s in particular were disastrous for the Aboriginal peoples.

Disease also contributed to the loss of the traditional Aboriginal way of life. Throughout the 1800s, measles, tuberculosis, and other diseases brought by fur traders, missionaries, and settlers killed many Aboriginal peoples.

Another serious problem was the presence of American whisky traders. The Americans traded whisky to the Aboriginal peoples in exchange for furs. Some of this alcohol was mixed with tobacco juice, red ink, and other ingredients that were harmful and sometimes fatal. When the Aboriginal peoples refused to trade, the American traders did not hesitate to kill them. Since there was no law enforcement in the region, the whisky traders built their own forts in the southern Prairies. Fort Whoop-Up, near present-day Lethbridge, flew the American flag.

The Aboriginal peoples were also concerned that settlers would take their lands. Like the Métis, they were not consulted when the Hudson's Bay Company sold Rupert's Land to Canada. During **treaty** negotiations a few years after the purchase, Chief Sweetgrass of the Plains Cree sent a message to the governor: "We heard our lands were sold and we did not like it; we don't want to sell our lands; it is our property, and no one has a right to sell them."

FURTHER UNDERSTANDING

Bison By the late 1800s, over-hunting meant that the destruction of the bison population had become a great concern. In addition to creating hunting regulations, the Canadian government sought other ways to protect the bison. In the early 1900s, the government bought several hundred bison from a Montana rancher and transformed them into preserves. These preserves included Wood Buffalo National Park, which straddles present-day Alberta and the Northwest Territories, and Elk Island Park, in present-day Alberta. Today, North America is home to between 80,000 and 100,000 bison.

Fort Whoop-Up John Healy and Alfred Hamilton, two Americans, set up Fort Whoop-Up in 1869 specifically for the whisky trade. Jerry Potts, a Métis, acted as a guide and interpreter for the North-West Mounted Police (NWMP) when they arrived in 1874. He helped them find Fort Whoop-Up. When illegal traders heard they were coming, the fort was abandoned. The NWMP then used it as one of their own posts.

■ Fort Whoop-Up was the most notorious of the several American whisky posts located in southern Alberta. Many of these whisky forts were given colourful names, such as "Whoop-Up" and "Robber's Roost."

Destruction of the Bison

Few disasters could compare to the destruction of the bison. The Aboriginal peoples of the Prairies depended on the bison for almost all their needs. Bison were their main source of food and the hides were used to provide shelter. From hoofs to horns, every part had a use. Without the bison, the prairie nations faced starvation.

A number of factors led to the near-extinction of the bison. Some people killed the bison for their hides, which made excellent leather and were in great demand by eastern factories. The growing industries needed leather for the pulleys and straps that drove machinery. Settlers killed the bison because they trampled crops and competed with livestock for food.

Repeat-action rifles, which did not have to be reloaded after every shot, allowed hunters to kill hundreds of animals in one hunt. Sportsmen took the train west and killed countless bison in the 1870s. "Buffalo Bill" Cody shot 500 bison in one day "just for fun." The record was 5,200 kills in one year. These men were not interested in the bison for food. After each hunt they left hundreds of rotting bison carcasses on the plains.

Finally, the Canadian government passed several laws to protect the bison, but by then it was nearly too late. In two decades, the number of bison had declined from millions to hundreds. In 1883, when a farmer in western Manitoba saw an old bison trotting across his land, it was reported in all the newspapers.

A SAD FAREWELL

One Cree leader mourned the destruction of the bison with a speech:

"Where are the bison? Where are our horses? They are gone, and we must soon follow them. These Prairies were ours once, and the bison were given to us by the Great Spirit. They kept us warm. They kept us from being hungry. They kept us in fuel. But they are all gone. Look at me. Look at those around me and say we look happy. Are these blankets warm enough for the winter? Are they like the bison robes we used to have? Let them send the bison back. Give us the Prairies again and we won't ask for food. But it is too late. It is too late."

■ The Plains nations had many rich traditions that they wanted to preserve, such as the importance of their healers.

Treaties and PROMISES

In Manitoba, the Salteaux forbade settlers to go beyond the Red River.

Before Macdonald's National Policy could proceed, he had to make sure the Aboriginal peoples would allow farmers to settle on their land. At this time, the American plains were the site of fierce wars between Aboriginal peoples and the United States army as settlers tried to take over Aboriginal lands. These wars cost the United States government about $20 million each year, which was more than the entire Canadian budget. Macdonald wanted to avoid a similar situation in Canada.

The Canadian Aboriginal peoples did not want to give up their lands. Many feared that their land would be stolen and that the settlers would destroy the bison. The Ojibwa tried to collect tolls from the immigrants who passed through their territory. In Manitoba, the Salteaux forbade settlers to go beyond the Red River. The Cree in Saskatchewan refused to allow government surveyors on their territory.

Some Aboriginal peoples agreed to allow settlers to enter the West if the government signed treaties with them. They wanted the government to recognize their entitlement to the land and to help them adjust to a new way of life. The Canadian government signed a series of treaties with the Aboriginal peoples on the Prairies. The Canadian government believed that the Aboriginal peoples who signed treaties should be bound by Canadian laws.

■ Chief Big Bear blamed the destruction of the Aboriginal way of life on the disappearance of the bison, European settlement, and treaty conditions.

FURTHER UNDERSTANDING

Big Bear Famine in the late 1870s forced some of the Plains Cree to sign Treaty Six in 1876. Big Bear and several other Plains Cree chiefs refused to sign because the treaty did not protect their laws and cultures. Big Bear reluctantly signed it in 1882 to save his people from starvation.

Big Bear wished to create a larger organization of Aboriginal peoples that would force Canada to renegotiate the earlier treaties and allow the Aboriginal peoples to hunt and live on their traditional territories. Some of Big Bear's former followers took a violent approach. Due to his association with them, Big Bear was found guilty of treason in 1885. He served two years of a three-year sentence.

THE NUMBERED TREATIES

Between 1871 and 1877, seven treaties were signed between the Canadian government and the Aboriginal peoples. Treaty One was intended for Aboriginal peoples of Lower Fort Garry. Sir Adams George Archibald, the first lieutenant-governor of Manitoba, explained to them: "Your Great Mother [Queen Victoria] wishes the good of all races under her sway. She wishes her … children to be happy and contented. She wishes them to live in comfort. She would like them to … till land and raise food and store it up against a time of want."

Although each treaty differed, the terms were generally the same. In return for their lands, each person received a small amount of money each year—about $5 to $12. The government also promised a certain amount of land to the Aboriginal peoples for reserves, as well as farm animals, agricultural equipment, schools, hunting supplies, and fishing and hunting rights. Another stipulation included the end of the liquor trade with Aboriginal peoples. Treaty Six specified that medicine and government assistance would be provided in the event of an epidemic.

It seemed, however, that both groups interpreted the treaties differently. Aboriginal peoples did not receive the help they expected, and at least one government official withheld assistance, expecting Aboriginal peoples to build homes first.

Aboriginal peoples were at a disadvantage. They were ravaged by epidemics, weakened by the whisky trade, and were losing their main food source, the bison. By this time, it was evident that non-Aboriginal people would continue to arrive and settle. While some Aboriginal peoples accepted the treaties as their best compromise within a limited range of possibilities, others, such as Big Bear, resisted. They did not want the government to control their lives.

■ The Numbered Treaties forced Peigan groups to agree to accept settlement on reserves. Permanent settlement on reserves meant that portable dwellings, such as teepees, a long-standing tradition, were no longer necessary.

The North-West Mounted POLICE

Constables earned $1 per day. They had to be physically fit and able to ride a horse.

Treaties alone were not enough. The West also needed law enforcement. In the early 1870s, the West was in turmoil. The dangerous brew supplied by American whisky traders led to violence and poverty around their forts. An outbreak of smallpox in 1870 killed approximately 3,500 Aboriginal peoples. Canadian settlers were increasingly fearful of the Aboriginal peoples, who in turn feared that the settlers would bring an end to their way of life. The Canadian government began to fear a general uprising by Aboriginal peoples.

To help solve these problems, Macdonald created the North-West Mounted Police (NWMP) in 1873. Lieutenant-Colonel George Arthur French was the first commissioner. The role of the force was to reassure the Aboriginal peoples of their rights, help the settlers, and maintain law and order in the West. The men wore scarlet tunics to remind the Aboriginal peoples of the British soldiers, with whom they had always had a good relationship.

Men who wanted to join the force had to be able to read and write either English or French, and have a good character. They had to be physically fit and able to ride a horse.

Constables earned $1 per day. Some were soldiers or had previous police experience, but others came from a variety of backgrounds, some having been farmers, tradesmen, clerks, and sailors. While most recruits came from Ontario, others came from Québec and the Maritimes.

Three hundred men were quickly trained in Winnipeg and, in 1874, they rode out on the Great March West. One group travelled 11,000 kilometres to

FURTHER UNDERSTANDING

Great March West The march westward took three months on horseback. On their way to Fort Whoop-Up, the NWMP hauled heavy carts loaded with supplies and munitions. It was a hot and dry summer, and this took its toll on the men and the horses and cattle they brought with them. In addition, swarms of black flies, flea infestations, severe prairie thunderstorms, low food rations, and dirty water resulted in slow progress— sometimes they travelled 20 kilometres or less in a day. They left dead horses on the trail and were forced to leave some equipment behind.

Eventually, Commissioner French divided the men, sending some along the well-worn route to Fort Edmonton. He was ordered to set up headquarters in Swan River. The Swan River Barracks served as the NWMP's headquarters from 1875 to 1876.

Lieutenant-Colonel James F. Macleod continued to Fort Whoop-Up. The first post was built at Fort Macleod in 1874 and the next year, Fort Calgary and Fort Walsh were established.

James F. Macleod James F. Macleod was the second NWMP commissioner, serving from 1876 to 1880. Fort Macleod, which he founded, was named in his honour. It served as the NWMP headquarters from 1876 to 1878. Macleod was also responsible for suppressing the whisky trade and negotiating an agreement with Blackfoot chiefs to finalize Treaty Seven. In 1887, he became a judge of the Supreme Court of the North-West Territories.

■ The red uniform of the "Mountie" was designed to distinguish them from the blue-jacketed U.S. Cavalry. For years, the cavalry had waged a bloody war against the Plains nations in the United States.

Lethbridge, and the other group went north to Edmonton. These 300 men were to police 6 million square kilometres.

The NWMP drove the whisky traders across the border, dealt fairly with the Aboriginal peoples, and developed a reputation for courage and honesty. In the early years, the NWMP often took the Aboriginal people's side against government agents. Crowfoot, the Blackfoot chief, said, "If the police had not come to the country, where would we all be now? Bad men and whisky were killing us so fast that very few of us would have been left today. The police have protected us as the feathers of the bird protect it from the frosts of winter."

The NWMP also helped the settlers. The men fought prairie fires, acted as health officers, conducted tours of the region for immigrants, patrolled the countryside, and visited settlers regularly.

SAM STEELE

Known as the "Lion of the Frontier," Sir Samuel Benfield Steele was a legendary figure in the history of western Canada. Steele was still in his early twenties when he enlisted with the newly created NWMP, having already helped turn back the Irish during the Fenian raids of 1866.

During his career, Steele arrested Louis Riel, single-handedly diffused a mob of protesting Canadian Pacific Railway (CPR) workers, worked nineteen-hour days to protect miners during the Klondike Gold Rush, and commanded Canadian forces in the Boer War. For his efforts, Steele was knighted by the King of England in 1918.

It was Steele's strength, courage, and determination during the NWMP's Great March West that first earned him recognition. Steele's diary of the trip provides an insight into the daily trials of this massive undertaking:

Some of the horses could not go on, and a marquee was pitched to shelter them at night, and two men were left in charge. Gagnon went ahead with the yoke oxen and was soon out of sight and I pushed with the horse teams and had the hardest trek that I have yet undertaken. The trail was worse than any we had encountered. It was knee-deep in black mud, sloughs crossed it every few hundred yards, and the wagons had to be unloaded and dragged through them by hand.

■ Fort Walsh was an NWMP base for five years and played an important role in preparing the Canadian West for peaceful settlement. A bustling frontier town sprang up near the fort.

A Transcontinental RAILWAY

No one knew if there was a route through the Rocky Mountains.

George-Étienne Cartier's offer in 1871 to complete a railway line to British Columbia in ten years had been rash. Few people had ever travelled overland from Ontario to the Pacific Ocean. The West had not been surveyed, and no one knew if there was a route through the Rocky Mountains.

By April 1872, Sir Sanford Fleming had selected a route across Canada. In 1873, the construction of the transcontinental railway was derailed by the Pacific Scandal, when the **Liberal** opposition discovered that the company awarded the contract to build the railway had given a great deal of money to the Conservative election campaign.

The scandal forced Macdonald's government to resign. A Liberal government under Alexander Mackenzie was elected in 1874. The Liberals, in power for the next five years, felt that private companies should be responsible for funding the construction of the railway. Unfortunately, the world was entering into an economic depression, and companies were not willing to take risks. Despite their own reservations, the Liberals felt the promise to British Columbia of a transcontinental railway would have to be honoured. Mackenzie decided that the railway's construction would be a government project.

Construction began in 1875 at Fort William, present-day Thunder Bay, Ontario. Sections of track were built in British Columbia, Manitoba, and north of Lake Superior. Mackenzie's railway was not truly transcontinental—the railway was to

FURTHER UNDERSTANDING

Sir Sanford Fleming Fleming surveyed potential routes for the CPR and was appointed engineer-in-chief in 1871. His other accomplishments included developing **Standard Time**, designing the first Canadian postage stamp, and promoting a telegraph line to connect Vancouver Island and Australia.

Pacific Scandal In 1872, the Conservatives accepted a large sum of money from Sir Hugh Allan to help win the election of 1872. In return for his gift, Allan expected the Conservatives to grant him the **charter** to build the transcontinental railway.

His plan failed because many people were afraid that if he was granted the charter, the railway would be controlled by Americans. Allan realized that the Canadian public and government would not tolerate this. He terminated his partnership with the Americans. In anger, they told the Liberal opposition of Allan's gift to the Conservatives. Although Allan was not granted the charter and Macdonald was not found guilty of accepting bribes, Parliament lost confidence in Macdonald and his government. He resigned as prime minister in November 1873.

William Van Horne Van Horne became general manager of the CPR in 1882. His energy and organizational skills led to the railway being completed ahead of schedule. Van Horne was a tireless worker who drove his men mercilessly. The labourers lived in cramped two-storey railway cars. Often working around the clock, 5,000 men and 1,700 teams of horses laid track across the Prairies in less than two years. He drove the last spike in 1885. In 1888, he became president of the CPR.

■ Sir Sanford Fleming worked for the railway when he arrived in Canada in 1845. Even after his retirement in 1880, he was still employed as a railway consultant.

link with bodies of water so that goods and people could be transferred from trains to boats, and back to trains again. Overall, little was accomplished until 1878, when Macdonald's Conservatives regained power. They returned to their policy of a route across Canada, but the government alone could not accomplish its construction.

The Canadian Pacific Railway

In 1880, George Stephen, a Montréaler, and his cousin from Winnipeg, Donald Smith, agreed to risk their personal fortunes and established the Canadian Pacific Railway Company (CPR). They were granted the contract to complete the route by 1891. In return, the company received $25 million, 1,012,145 hectares of farmland—which the CPR later sold—10 million hectares of land adjacent to the tracks, 1,127 kilometres of government-owned portions of railway worth $37 million, and a railway monopoly for twenty years. Even so, the company directors had to go into debt to finish the railway.

William Van Horne was hired to oversee the construction. It was easy to lay track on the flat, open Prairies in comparison to the land north of Lake Superior, which consisted of granite, fast-flowing rivers, tall forests, and muskeg. One stretch of muskeg swallowed the track seven times, and even covered three locomotives. Black flies and mosquitoes drove the men crazy.

■ The Canadian Pacific Railway would eventually cross 5,000 kilometres of territory and would become the longest railway on Earth.

CONSTRUCTION
in British Columbia

The Rocky Mountains presented the greatest challenge to those laying track. Andrew Onderdonk led the railway builders in the Fraser Canyon in present-day British Columbia. First, they had to blast a path through the rock to lay track. Men had to be lowered on ropes down the slippery canyon walls. Then, often barefoot for balance, they carefully drilled holes into the rock for the dynamite charges before being hauled back to the top. The fuses were lit, and everyone ran for safety. Some men were killed when a secondary explosion went off, or when a piece of rock flew straight into their hiding place. Fatal accidents occurred when workers were not careful while handling dynamite. Mud and rock slides also claimed many lives.

One year after he arrived, Onderdonk was finally ready to start laying track, but he needed many more men.

Impact of the Railway

The railway tracks slowly crept north up the canyon. Within five years, a transcontinental railway, that was 3,219 kilometres long, was finished. In November 1885, construction crews met to watch Van Horne pound the last spike in Eagle Pass.

The railway was two-thirds longer than any other railway in the world. Its completion was an engineering miracle and had a tremendous impact on the West. The railway brought many new settlers. The non-Aboriginal population in the West mushroomed from 1,000 in 1870 to 50,000 twenty years later. Cities such as Regina, Moose Jaw, Medicine Hat, and Calgary appeared almost overnight along the main line. As Chief Poundmaker told his people in 1882, "Next summer, or at the latest next fall, the railway will be close to us, the whites will fill the country, and they will dictate to us as they please. It is useless to dream that we can frighten them, that time is passed."

FURTHER UNDERSTANDING

Andrew Onderdonk Andrew Onderdonk was an engineer with the skills and financial backing to tackle the route through the Rocky Mountains. He soon realized that it cost too much to move supplies along the Caribou Road by wagon train. He decided that he would try to bring a steamship to the Upper Fraser River through a dangerous passage known as Hell's Gate. Onderdonk had the workers drive ring bolts into the walls of the canyon. Then, workers pulled ropes that were threaded through the rings and attached to the steamship. With much muscle power, the steamship eventually made it through the passage.

■ After the departure of the dignitaries, the remaining workers posed for their own version of the last spike ceremony. The end piece of the final rail and the last tie were chipped away for souvenirs.

THE CHINESE WORKERS

Onderdonk brought many Chinese north from California and China to help build the railway. Men from China were willing to travel to North America, where they might earn enough money to provide for their families. The typical sum was $300. Once he had saved this much, a man would return home.

The Chinese were not popular with the other people of the province. It was feared that the Chinese would take all the jobs. Some said that the Chinese—who worked for one-half to one-third less wages—would drive pay scales down so that Canadian labourers could not earn a living. The Chinese also had to deal with racism among many of their co-workers.

The Chinese proved they were hard workers; they did not quit their jobs. They were selected for the tough and dangerous jobs—the blasting and digging. Hundreds of Chinese men died in accidents on the job.

Eventually, the politicians of British Columbia eventually passed laws to keep the Chinese from entering the province. The Canadian government in Ottawa overruled these laws because the railway was more important than the complaints of the citizens of British Columbia.

It was not easy for the Chinese to save $300. By the time they had paid their board out of their small wages, they could rarely save more than $40 a year. Construction on the railway would be over long before their savings added up to the required amount.

■ Approximately 15,000 Chinese labourers worked to complete the British Columbian section of the CPR. More than 600 Chinese labourers died on the job.

INJUSTICE on the Plains

By the early 1880s, the people of the Plains nations were concerned that the government was not meeting the terms of their treaties. Agricultural supplies and breeding stock were often slow to arrive or of poor quality. There was disagreement and confusion about the size and location of reserves. The Aboriginal peoples felt that the treaties should include everything that had been discussed, not only what had been written down.

The Canadian government appointed agents to turn the Aboriginal peoples into "Canadians." Agents forbade the Aboriginals their traditional celebrations and dances, such as the Sun Dance. Agents took Aboriginal children from their parents and placed them in residential schools. Only Aboriginal people who left their reserve and gave up their Aboriginal status were eligible to vote. Aboriginal women who married non-Aboriginal men lost their treaty rights.

An economic depression began in the early 1880s. The Canadian government cut back on its rations to the Aboriginal peoples. One government inspector reported, "There is a great deal of misery in all the camps. The old women and children are housed in wretched lodges, which are no protection whatever in cold weather. At present I am giving them ninety sacks of flour per week and about a similar amount of meat. They are thus receiving two days' food to last them for seven days." Between 1880 and 1885, the Aboriginal population declined from 32,000 to 20,000.

FURTHER UNDERSTANDING

Gabriel Dumont Gabriel Dumont's grandfather was a French-Canadian **voyageur**. His grandmother was Sarcee. As a boy, Dumont went on the annual bison hunts. By 20 years of age, he was an excellent horseman and could handle his rifle well. He spoke French and six Aboriginal languages, but never learned to read or write.

Following the Red River Resistance in 1869, settlers from Ontario poured into Manitoba. Dumont and his wife sold their land cheaply, moved to the Métis settlement of St. Laurent in 1872, and farmed. Gabriel had to travel long distances to locate bison. His last hunt was in 1880. In Métis settlements, the people elected their own government. Dumont became president, and, together with other officials, made laws for the community.

Red River Resistance
In 1869, prior to Canada's purchase of Rupert's Land from the Hudson's Bay Company, the government sent surveyors to divide the land. Concerned that their traditional lands were being taken from them, the Métis resisted the efforts of the surveyors.

Under the leadership of Louis Riel, the Métis established a temporary government to negotiate with Canada. They drafted a List of Rights and presented it to the Canadian government. Eventually, Prime Minister Sir John A. Macdonald agreed to the majority of the terms in the List of Rights. The Red River Resistance resulted in the creation of the province of Manitoba, through the Manitoba Act of 1870.

Residential schools At these church-run boarding schools, students learned English, Christianity, and farming. This was one method of assimilating Aboriginal peoples into the growing non-Aboriginal population.

■ Chief Crowfoot of the Blackfoot maintained positive relationships with the fur traders and the NWMP. In 1885, he forbade his people to partake in the North-West Rebellion.

The Aboriginal peoples renewed their efforts to create a territory that would be under their control. In 1884, Chiefs Big Bear and Poundmaker called a meeting of the Plains Cree. Both men believed that violence would end in failure. They decided to unite in their demands of the government. "Long before the Palefaces," Big Bear said to an agent, "this vast land was the hunting ground of my people … This fair land is now the land of the white man—the land of the stranger. Our big game is no more."

Métis Concerns

By the early 1880s, Métis such as Gabriel Dumont were concerned about their land. The Canadian Pacific Railway reached Calgary in 1883. The arrival of Canadian settlers reminded the Métis of the troubles experienced in 1869, during the Red River Resistance. They had no legal proof that the land was theirs. Aboriginal peoples had been given reserves, but the Métis had not.

When the Canadian government began to survey the land, tension increased. The Métis held mass meetings. They sent petitions to Ottawa. Macdonald's government ignored their pleas. By 1884, the Métis were growing desperate.

Settlers' Demands

The settlers were also unhappy with Ottawa. The Canadian Pacific Railway charged too much to ship grain east. The tariffs increased the price of manufactured goods. Many people had wanted the railway to go through Battleford and Edmonton. Instead, it followed a southern route through Regina and Calgary.

In addition, the settlers were angry that so much farmland had been given to the Hudson's Bay Company and the Canadian Pacific Railway. They believed that the Canadian government favoured central Canada over western Canada. The settlers demanded changes in government that would give them greater control of their own affairs.

■ Before the North-West Rebellion, Gabriel Dumont operated the local ferry and owned a small store in Batoche.

The North-West REBELLION

In 1884, the Métis met with the settlers near Prince Albert to discuss their problems. They decided, at Gabriel Dumont's suggestion, to invite Louis Riel to the West. Riel had been successful in 1869; perhaps he could repeat this success. Riel agreed to return: "Fifteen years ago, I gave my heart to my nation," he declared. "I am ready to give it again."

Riel Returns

Riel spoke to the settlers and the English-speaking Métis about the need for united action to bring about change. However, Riel secretly wrote to Macdonald promising either to leave the country or to make the Métis do what the government wanted in return for money. Macdonald refused.

Next, Riel met with the Aboriginal peoples, who were angry that the Canadian government had not lived up to its treaty promises. The Métis, the Aboriginal peoples, and the settlers agreed that they had the same goals and wanted to achieve them peacefully. They drew up a petition in December 1884 and sent it to Ottawa.

The people waited for the Canadian government to respond. Many people warned Macdonald that there could be violence if the complaints were ignored. Finally, the prime minister promised to look into the situation, but nothing was done.

■ In 1875, Louis Riel suffered a nervous breakdown and was admitted to a hospital at Longue Pointe in Montréal.

FURTHER UNDERSTANDING

Father Lacombe Father Lacombe was a missionary to both the Cree and the Blackfoot. He ministered in present-day Alberta and started a mission called St. Albert in the early 1860s. He was trusted and respected by the Métis and the Aboriginal peoples, who called him "The Man of the Good Heart." Upon hearing of Riel's arrival and of unrest among the Métis, he wrote to warn Macdonald of possible trouble:

I blame the Métis and I have not spared them reproaches. But I will permit myself to say to Your Honour with all possible respect, that the Canadian Government is itself not free of blame …

Louis Riel The previous fourteen years had changed Riel. After fleeing Red River in 1870, Riel lived as a fugitive. The Red River Métis elected him to Parliament three times, but there was a reward out for his capture, so Riel did not dare take his seat. He spent much of his time travelling between Canada and the United States.

During his exile, Riel became lonely and frustrated. He dreamed of creating a new church in which the Métis were the chosen people and he was the prophet. He wished to change the Sabbath from Sunday to Saturday. His Roman Catholic friends in Montréal believed that he had lost his mind, and placed him in a mental institution. Released in 1878, Riel went to the United States. He married a Métis woman and had two children. In 1884, Riel was employed as a schoolteacher in a Jesuit mission in Montana.

Conflict Begins

Riel decided to use the same tactics that had been successful at Red River. On March 19, he created a temporary government at Batoche in the hope that Macdonald would negotiate with the Métis. Such a tactic seemed certain to lead to violence, and the settlers and Catholic clergy refused to support him.

One week later, an NWMP force, together with civilian volunteers, set out to arrest Riel. It was defeated at Duck Lake by a group of Métis under Dumont's leadership. On April 1, 1885, some of Big Bear's warriors attacked the settlement at Frog Lake. Big Bear tried to stop the attack, but he could not. About ten days later, some of Big Bear's warriors surrounded Fort Pitt. This time, Big Bear was able to prevent bloodshed. He sent a note to Fort Pitt warning the people to escape.

Meanwhile, a large number of Cree and Assiniboine held Fort Battleford under siege for nearly a month. They easily defeated the military force that tried to subdue them, and Chief Poundmaker barely managed to keep his group from pursuing the fleeing soldiers.

Rumours spread that a full-scale uprising was about to begin, but most Aboriginal peoples kept their treaty promise not to break the peace. Macdonald sent food to these people to ensure that they remained neutral. The Blackfoot Nation did not join Riel partly because the Catholic missionary, Father Lacombe, had influence over their chief, Crowfoot.

■ The government used the Canadian Pacific Railway to transport 3,000 troops west to quell the North-West Rebellion.

Government Troops Head **WEST**

Within ten days of the Duck Lake battle, the Canadian government had moved 3,000 troops west.

Riel had miscalculated. The situation in the West was not the same as it had been in 1869. The NWMP were already on hand to defend against uprisings. Telegraph wires now provided instant communication with central Canada. Most importantly, the CPR now extended from Winnipeg to Calgary. Within ten days of the Duck Lake battle, the Canadian government had moved 3,000 troops west.

The Métis were no match for the Canadian soldiers under General Frederick Middleton. Not only did the soldiers greatly outnumber the few hundred Métis fighters, they also had cannons, better rifles, and a Gatling gun that fired 1,000 shots a minute.

The Battle of Batoche

The Métis' best tactic was **guerrilla warfare**, and Dumont was an expert at this type of fighting. However, Riel told Dumont to wait until the soldiers attacked first.

The final battle took place at Batoche in early May, 1885. Batoche fell and Riel surrendered on May 15, three days after the battle. Poundmaker and the Battleford Cree surrendered on May 26. Big Bear and his people fought two more skirmishes. When Big Bear turned himself in to the NWMP on July 2, the rebellion was over.

Results of the Rebellion

After the rebellion, many people were arrested and charged with treason-felony, which was not as serious as the charge against Riel—high treason. Eighteen Métis were sentenced to prison terms ranging from one to seven years. Eight Cree men were hanged for their part in the Frog Lake incident. Poundmaker and Big Bear were each sentenced to three years in prison.

The government took advantage of the conflict to break promises with the Aboriginal peoples who opposed its plans to end their independence. The prison

FURTHER UNDERSTANDING

Batoche To prepare for the NWMP, the Métis dug trenches around the village of Batoche. Ammunition and guns were in short supply in the Métis trenches. The defenders held out as long as they could. On the fourth day, the Canadian forces charged, and the Métis surrendered.

General Frederick Middleton Frederick Middleton was a British officer who came to Canada in 1868. He became Commander of the Canadian Militia in 1884. He received a promotion, a medal, and money in recognition of his leadership during the North-West Rebellion.

Thomas Scott In 1870, during the Red River Resistance, Thomas Scott was tried for treason by the temporary Métis government. He was found guilty of violence and hostility against the prison guards and the Métis government. His death by firing squad divided the country.

■ The Battle of Batoche ended the North-West Rebellion. After three days of fighting, General Frederick Middleton's force of 900 troops defeated the 300 Métis and Aboriginal defenders.

terms given to Big Bear and Poundmaker deprived the Aboriginal peoples of their leadership. The government took their horses and guns, and divided the nations they considered troublesome. The Plains people were now almost entirely dependent upon government assistance.

Some of the Métis fled farther west, hoping to escape the advancing settlers. Forced to abandon their old lifestyle, many Métis took odd jobs in the cities.

THE TRIAL OF LOUIS RIEL

During the summer of 1885, Louis Riel's trial in Regina made newspaper headlines across the country. The penalty for high treason was death.

Riel's lawyers were not allowed to discuss the Métis grievances that led to rebellion because the judge ruled that the government was not on trial. The defence lawyers tried to argue that Riel was not guilty by virtue of insanity, but Riel disagreed with them. If he were judged insane, it would imply that the Métis had not been justified in rebelling. The jury met for one hour before deciding Riel was guilty. The jury recommended mercy, but the judge ruled that Riel would be hanged.

The verdict caused a split between British and French Canadians. During the rebellion, French Canadians had not supported Riel's actions. In fact, two French-Canadian battalions fought under General Middleton. However, French Canadians now demanded that Macdonald cancel the death sentence and commit Riel to a mental institution. British Canadians demanded that Riel hang. Some still felt that Riel should be punished for Thomas Scott's death.

Macdonald twice postponed the execution and had Riel examined by doctors. They thought he had strange political and religious ideas, but that he could tell right from wrong and was therefore legally sane. Macdonald agreed and Riel was hanged on November 16, 1885.

■ The trial of Louis Riel lasted two weeks. The jury that decided that Louis Riel was guilty consisted of six English-speaking Protestants.

The First Canadian
ADMINISTRATIONS

Sir John A. Macdonald's First Term as Prime Minister (1867–1873)

1869	Canada purchases Rupert's Land from the Hudson's Bay Company
1870	Manitoba becomes a province; the remaining territory becomes the North-West Territories
1871	British Columbia joins Canada
1871–1877	Seven treaties called the "Numbered Treaties," are signed with the Aboriginal peoples
1873	The North-West Mounted Police is established
	Prince Edward Island joins Canada
	The Pacific Scandal occurs and Macdonald resigns

■ Alexander Mackenzie

Alexander Mackenzie Forms Canada's First Liberal Administration (1873–1878)

1874	The Royal Military College is established
1875	The Supreme Court of Canada is established
	Construction of the Canadian Pacific Railway begins
1876	The Indian Act is passed
1878	Secret ballot is introduced as an election practice
	Mackenzie is defeated by Macdonald due to support for Macdonald's National Policy

Sir John A. Macdonald's Second Term as Prime Minister (1878–1891)

1879	Tariff protection is put into effect
1880s	The Canadian government overrules British Columbia's laws intended to stop Chinese people from entering the province
	Aboriginal, Métis, and settler discontent
1880	The Canadian Pacific Railway Company is established
	Britain gives Canada control of the Arctic Islands
1885	The Canadian Pacific Railway is completed
	The North-West Rebellion occurs
1891	Macdonald wins a tough election, but dies shortly thereafter

A Backdrop for
REBELLION

CAUSES

- Aboriginal population is weakened by whisky trade, disease, declining numbers of bison, and hunger
- Aboriginal peoples are dissatisfied as the Canadian government is not fulfilling treaty terms
- Government agents try to "Canadianize" Aboriginal peoples
- Canadian Pacific Railway brings more settlers west
- Métis grow increasingly concerned about land rights and the preservation of their culture
- Canadian surveyors arrive on Métis land

EVENTS

- Louis Riel is asked back by the Métis
- Riel meets with Métis, Aboriginal peoples, and settlers. They draft a petition to the government outlining demands, but the government is slow to respond
- Riel establishes a temporary government
- The Canadian government sends a force to arrest Riel; the force is defeated at Duck Lake under Dumont's leadership
- Warriors attack Frog Lake settlement
- The Cree and the Assiniboine hold Fort Battleford under siege and defeat the military force
- 3,000 NWMP head west under General Frederick Middleton's command
- NWMP defeat Riel, Dumont, and the Métis at Batoche
- Riel, Poundmaker, Big Bear, and the Battleford Cree surrender

RESULTS

- Rebels are charged with treason-felony; Riel is convicted of high treason and hanged
- Verdict creates division between French and British Canadians
- Big Bear and Poundmaker are jailed; their people are deprived of leadership
- The Government takes horses and guns, and divides "troublesome" nations
- Plains people now depend upon government assistance
- The Government breaks promises made to the Aboriginal peoples
- The Métis flee west and are forced to abandon their traditional way of life

Settling the WEST

The population of the West increased much more slowly than Macdonald hoped. Conflicts with the Métis and Aboriginal peoples hindered settlement. Grasshopper plagues, drought, and low prices for farm products further discouraged immigration to the Canadian West. Only a few settlers came, mostly from Ontario, the United States, Russia, and Iceland.

A Population Explosion

When Wilfrid Laurier became prime minister in 1896, he was determined to settle the West. He appointed Clifford Sifton as the minister in charge of immigration. Sifton launched a huge advertising campaign to attract settlers from Britain, the American West, and Europe. Now, Canada had better transportation, and the market for agricultural produce had improved. In addition, the United States was discouraging immigrants.

The results were staggering. Between 1901 and 1906, Calgary's population grew from 4,100 to 12,000, and Edmonton's population increased from 2,600 to 11,200. Immigrants came from many countries around the world including Sweden, India, Denmark, Germany, Japan, Italy, Russia, and China. More than 1 million immigrants came from Great Britain. Overcrowding, poverty, and unemployment in Britain encouraged many people to start life anew in North America.

Approximately 500,000 people came from the United States. Many of these people were from minority groups such as the Mormons and Hutterites, and sought to escape **persecution**. More than 700,000

FURTHER UNDERSTANDING

Clifford Sifton Clifford Sifton was born in Ontario in 1861. Sifton moved to Manitoba in 1875 and began practicing law. In 1896, he made the switch to federal politics and played an essential role in Laurier's liberal government. His policy of attracting homesteaders from Eastern Europe angered many British Canadians, who thought the West should be settled by English-speaking citizens. In 1898, he purchased the *Manitoba Free Press*, through which he voiced his political opinions. Sifton retired from politics in 1911, and was knighted in 1915.

■ In the late 1890s, Clifford Sifton began a massive advertising campaign aimed at convincing European peasants to immigrate to Canada. Sifton's program was extremely successful and continued to attract settlers long after he left politics.

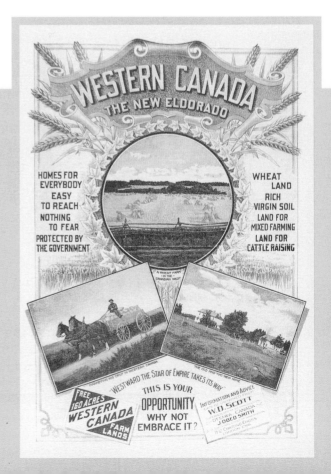

immigrants came from Russia and central Europe. Ukrainians, Poles, Doukhobors, and Slavs from Austria-Hungary came to Canada to escape religious persecution and the harsh life in their homelands. Chinese and Japanese came to British Columbia, where they helped construct railways and other public works.

The rapid population growth inspired great optimism in Canada. The arrival of about 2 million people from around the world transformed Canada into a multicultural society.

HOMESTEADING IN THE WEST

This account of homesteading in the West was written by an unidentified woman. Her father had travelled through the Canadian and American West before deciding to homestead on land near Calgary. She describes her experiences when her family moved to Calgary because crops in North Dakota had been poor for several years:

Eleven of us set out for Calgary. There was Grandmother, my parents, and eight of the ten children. We hadn't gone more than 160 kilometres when the younger fry shrieked with delight at some hills in southern Manitoba, thinking they were the Rocky Mountains and that Calgary was just around the corner.

As there were no beds on the train we slept as best we could on the seats. At last, in the early morning of the third day, we arrived in Calgary. Those were the horse-and-buggy days. There were no automobiles of any kind, no street-cars, no buses, only vehicles pulled by horses.

Eighth Avenue was called Stephen Avenue, and was the main street. It was not paved. Instead of parking meters, there were hitching-posts where the drivers could fasten their horses. The only "speeding" was when a horse, frightened by a strange noise, broke loose and ran wildly down the street. Noise pollution in these days consisted chiefly of the rattle of cart wheels. The "sky-scrapers," if you could call them that, were at most five or six storeys high.

The southern limit of the city was 17th Avenue. We liked the beautiful blue skies with the lovely white clouds so high above, and we loved the sunshine. Many a time we said: "Thank God for Sunny Alberta!"

■ Early settlers of the West often lived in tar-paper shacks and sod huts. However, it did not take long for the Prairie settlements to develop.

Canada's Industrial REVOLUTION

Since factories could mass-produce goods for low prices, big industries put small craftspeople out of business.

The protective tariffs created by Sir John A. Macdonald's government encouraged Canadians to start their own factories. American businesses also built branch plants to produce goods in Canada and to avoid paying high import duties. Most of the factories were set up in Québec and Ontario. Factories produced pulp and paper, boots and shoes, agricultural implements, and textiles. Mines produced copper, iron, coal, and nickel. The first steel plant in Canada was built at Trenton, Nova Scotia, and another was built near the Cape Breton coal fields. Soon, Nova Scotia produced half of Canada's steel, but most of the factories that used it were located in central Canada.

This was a good time for business people to get rich. Wages were low and unions were not very powerful. There was no income tax. Since factories could mass-produce goods for low prices, big industries put small craftspeople out of business. Storekeepers became frustrated by the number of people who ordered cheaper goods from popular mail-order catalogues.

Immigrants continued to pour into Western Canada. Western farmers produced record amounts of grain and dairy products. In the last half of the nineteenth century, rural areas of Québec and Ontario suffered from poor crops, high prices for goods, and low prices for crops. Many people gave up farming there to head west or to the United States.

As steamships replaced the great sailing ships of the 1800s, the shipbuilding and

FURTHER UNDERSTANDING

Unions A group of workers form a union by organizing to ensure that their rights in the workplace are protected. Many workers together have a stronger voice than one worker alone when negotiations take place. Worker demands might include increased wages or better working conditions, such as a reasonable limit on the number of hours worked per day. In 1872, workers from various places in Canada participated in the "Nine-hour Movement," an effort to reduce the work day from twelve to nine hours. The Trades Union Act was passed in 1872. Though some employers resisted unions, the late 1800s saw many demonstrations and strikes.

■ Large department stores first appeared during Canada's Industrial Revolution. Robert Simpson's store in downtown Toronto was founded in 1872.

forestry industries in the Maritimes faded away. Thousands of Maritimers left their homes for greener pastures in the United States or Western Canada.

Labour Conditions

In the late 1800s, low-paying factory jobs became available. The factory system tried to get the most out of employees by increasing the pace and limiting the skills the worker required. Adults worked ten to twelve hours per day, six days a week. Companies could require their workers to work overtime with no notice and no extra pay. Lunch lasted thirty minutes, and at busy times, meals were eaten in the factory. In the winter, smoke from lamps and coal stoves made it difficult to see across the room. There were no hospital insurance plans, sick benefits, or compensation for workers hurt in accidents, even though machinery caused many injuries. Workers in small towns were often required to spend part of their wages in the over-priced company store, or to pay high rent for poor housing. Some businesses closed up without paying their employees.

ORGANIZED LABOUR

A few unions were started in Canada during the early 1800s. In the beginning, they were small and often illegal. Union members could be imprisoned, but they persisted in trying to get better conditions for workers. In the 1870s, there were several strikes in Ontario's industrial towns and in Montréal. After a strike by Toronto printers, the government passed the Trade Unions Act, which stated that unions were not illegal conspiracies. The Royal Commission on the Relations of Labour and Capital supported the need for unions. It stated that the person who sells his labour should be considered equal to the person buying it.

However, this did not grant the unions any more power. Owners fired workers who joined unions. During strikes, the courts and the government favoured the owners over the workers. A large number of immigrants were looking for work and there were no minimum-wage laws. This allowed the factory and mine owners to pay low wages and hire strike breakers when needed. When all else failed, the Mounted Police or the militia were used to break strikes.

■ In the late 1800s, only 10 percent of Canadian workers had a union to represent them.

LIFESTYLES at the
Turn of the Century

At the turn of the twentieth century, telephones provided instant communication throughout North America. In 1901, St. John's, Newfoundland, received the first transatlantic wireless message from Britain. The following year, an underwater cable connected Vancouver to Australia. Other Canadian firsts included the motion picture camera, safety razors, electric stoves, cash registers, and vacuum cleaners.

The Upper Class

There was an enormous gap between rich and poor. The wealthiest business people lived in huge mansions, complete with stained glass windows, immense ballrooms, elevators, and fountains. Their homes had electric lights, running water, indoor plumbing, telephones, icebox refrigerators, carpet sweepers, gas ranges, hand-cranked washing machines, and servants.

The upper- and middle-class men joined sporting clubs and participated in a wide variety of games. Winning was less important than how the game was played. Sports taught discipline, teamwork, honesty, and persistence. The leaders of society opposed professional sports because they believed that sports should be a minor aspect of life, not a full-time occupation. Many did not want the working classes competing against them and joining their private clubs.

The Working Classes

Seasonal workers and the unemployed lived in cramped and unsafe slums. Their children wore ragged clothes and begged for pennies on street corners. Some children sold newspapers on the main streets, or shined shoes. To survive, many families took in boarders and raised pigs in the backyard.

FURTHER UNDERSTANDING

Infant mortality A common measure of death rate, or mortality, is the number of deaths per thousand people in the population. Infant mortality is a measure of the number of baby deaths within the first year of life. At the turn of the twentieth century, one of every ten babies, or 10 percent of babies, did not survive the first year.

■ Many people in the working classes lived in slum conditions. Eventually, the government promoted the construction of new houses, the repair and modernization of existing houses, and the general improvement of community environments.

Most people who were born into poverty stayed there, as did their children. To be successful in business, a person required money, the right contacts, proper manners, and education. Poor parents could not afford to send their children to school for very long.

Health

In the last quarter of the nineteenth century, microscopes helped identify bacteria. Scientists discovered that germs were the cause of typhoid, leprosy, malaria, tuberculosis, tetanus, cholera, and diphtheria. As a result of this discovery, an emphasis on cleanliness, the use of face masks and rubber surgical gloves, and the sterilization of surgical instruments improved patients' chances of survival.

Open sewers, polluted drinking water, poor nutrition, and overcrowded homes brought sickness and death to many, especially to children and poor people. The major cause of death was tuberculosis. Heart disease, a leading cause of death today, was responsible for less than 4 percent of all deaths in 1900. The infant mortality rate was high.

A WORLD OF WHEELS

By the end of the nineteenth century, the world seemed much smaller than it did thirty years earlier. Steamships journeyed to all corners of the earth. Electric streetcars provided rapid, convenient transportation within the larger Canadian cities, and railways linked communities. The first airplane flight in the world took place in 1903, and the first flight in Canada was only 6 years later.

The development of the modern bicycle provided cheap and popular transportation. Telegraph messengers sped down roads to deliver telegrams. Doctors rode bicycles to house calls.

Labourers rode to work, and letter carriers delivered the mail by bike. Although women wearing **bloomers** for bicycle riding shocked many people, bloomers allowed more freedom and comfort and eventually led to the wearing of shorter skirts for athletics.

The motor car became popular in the first decade of the twentieth century. It was expensive, noisy, and frequently broke down. Early models were started by hand-cranks, had no windshields, and suffered flat tires every few kilometres. For many years, the car was used more for pleasure than for work. In Calgary, men could buy a driver's license at age 16 and women at age 18. In 1907, the Calgary City Council set the speed limit at 16 kilometres per hour. Since there were no stop signs or traffic lights, drivers had to slow down to 8 kilometres per hour at intersections.

■ Apartment buildings became popular in Canada during the nineteenth century. They were most popular with the emerging middle class.

CHILDREN in Canada

In the mid-nineteenth century, most people thought of children as miniature adults who needed discipline to prevent them from doing evil. Psychologists said that children were like pieces of clay that could be molded any way the parents wished. Near the end of the century, however, children were viewed more like plants that needed careful tending and nurturing. People now believed that the children were the country's future.

Governments passed new laws to protect children. Children under 16 years of age were forbidden to enter pool rooms and no one under 18 years of age could buy tobacco. In the 1870s, owing largely to the efforts of Egerton Ryerson, provinces began to pass laws that made attendance at school compulsory.

Several cities established separate children's courts. The Ontario Juvenile Act stated, "Every juvenile delinquent shall be treated, not as a criminal, but as a misdirected and misguided child." The Children's Aid Society was created to protect children from drunken and cruel parents.

FURTHER UNDERSTANDING

Egerton Ryerson Ryerson became superintendent of education in Canada West in 1846. He studied the education systems of other countries, such as the United States, as well as in Europe, and then developed and promoted his ideas for Canada. He supported the idea of compulsory, free, and universal education.

Compulsory meant required attendance. Universal meant that every citizen of eligible school-age would have access to an education because the education system would be publicly funded. It would also be controlled by the government. This would include maintaining curriculum, textbook, and teacher training standards. The School Act of 1871 established universal education in Ontario. All children had to attend school until they were 12 years old, and they could no longer sell newspapers or polish shoes on city streets. Other provinces soon followed Ontario's example.

Child Labour

Near the end of the 1800s, many children worked full time in factories. They did simple, boring tasks, and worked between sixty and seventy-two hours each week, the same hours as adults. Children were hired instead of adults because they did not complain and they could be paid less. The average factory salary was $8.50 per week for men, $4.00 for women, and $1.50 for children.

Some provinces passed laws to protect children. In 1884, Ontario forbade factories from hiring boys under 12 years of age and girls under the age of 14. Nova Scotia forbade children under 12 from working underground in the mines. Québec set the minimum working age at 13. These laws, however, were poorly enforced. In 1891, 75,000 children aged 10 to 14 still worked full time.

Those children who arrived late for work, talked on the job, or otherwise misbehaved were fined, beaten, or temporarily locked up.

■ Until the late eighteenth century, it was generally assumed that from about age 7, children should contribute to the family economy. Many children worked in dangerous coal mines.

WOMEN in Canada

Women's choices in society were limited at the turn of the century. They were not allowed in bowling alleys or taverns, and could not go to a theatre alone. When the Toronto Library opened in 1882, several people campaigned to ban fiction books. They believed that sensational tales of women marrying rich men and leaving for exotic places would make women unhappy with their role in Canadian society. Divorce was rare. Between 1867 and 1901, there were only fifty-three divorces in Canada.

At the time, society considered women to be morally superior to men, and men to be physically and intellectually stronger than women. Schools had separate playgrounds and entrances for each gender, and girls' exercises were much easier than those for boys. Some people believed that women were too emotional and weak for the harsh realities of life outside the home, and that too much thinking might destroy a woman's brain. It was felt that women belonged in the home, in the role of mother and wife. Society feared that if women went to work, children would be neglected, the home would be forgotten, and the family would break apart. Businessmen's wives were expected to direct the servants' work and occupy themselves with fashions and by entertaining friends.

> Some people believed that too much thinking might destroy a woman's brain.

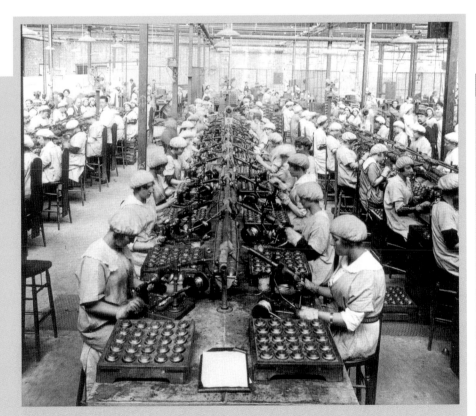

■ During World War I, women replaced male factory workers who had joined the armed services. At the end of the war, women were strongly encouraged to leave the work force. Married women employed by the government were forced to leave.

FURTHER UNDERSTANDING

Women's fashion Upper- and middle-class women wore lace, silk, velvet, or satin dresses. They brushed their hair forward from the back and held it in place on top with hair pins. Ostrich feathers were attached to their hats. In 1890, the fashionable woman wore an average of 17 kilograms of clothes in the winter. By 1900, however, women began to experiment with two-piece outfits with narrower sleeves and fewer bustles. According to the Paris fashion designers, the ideal waist was 46 centimetres. Many women fainted trying to pull their corsets tight enough to meet these standards. Dresses were tight at the hips and flared to the ground in a bell shape so as not to reveal the shape of the thigh. Women who played sports wore skirts that reached the ankles.

WOMEN at Work

Whatever career choice a woman made, she was subjected to long hours, low pay, and strict discipline.

Although some new conveniences made housework easier, it was still a difficult chore. Coal and wood stoves were dirty and awkward to manage. Laundry was done with washboards and hand wringers. Irons were heated and reheated on the stove. Most women made their own clothes, bread, and preserves.

Despite society's objections, many women had to work outside the home. The only jobs women were considered able to perform were in the public and domestic services, working as maids, teachers, or nurses. The largest number of women worked as domestic servants. These young women, many of whom were recent immigrants, spent their days cleaning other women's houses and looking after their children. Clerical and sales jobs were just beginning to open up for women, who were considered more polite than men and were willing to work for lower wages.

Since teaching and nursing were thought to be part of a mother's role, these occupations were dominated by women. At the turn of the century, three out of every four teachers were women. However, women teachers were paid less than males, could not become principals, and were generally confined to elementary schools.

By 1900, women made up one-quarter of the manufacturing work force. As factories opened, it became acceptable for women to work on the assembly lines. These women were paid only half the salary men earned. Whatever career choice a woman made, she was subjected to long hours, low pay, and strict discipline.

The University of Toronto did not admit women until the 1880s. Most professions were still closed to women. People would not accept the idea that women could perform the jobs as well as men. Against the odds, women slowly began to enter professions once reserved for men.

FURTHER UNDERSTANDING

Professions Occupations which require special training, such as law and medicine, are called professions. In 1891, Carrie Derick became the first female professor in Canada, and twelve years later, Emma Baker became the first woman to earn a Ph.D. Cora Hind in Winnipeg and Kit Coleman in Toronto proved that women could be excellent journalists. In 1895, Clara Brett Martin became Canada's first woman law graduate. When Grace Annie Lockhart graduated from Mount Allison, New Brunswick in 1875, she became the first woman in the **British Empire** to receive a university degree. Women made slower progress in Québec, where they were forbidden to practice law until 1941.

One woman had to disguise herself to enter her profession of choice. Dr. James Barry was born in Scotland, and, as a young girl, longed to be a doctor. Since women were not admitted to medical school at the University of Edinburgh, she disguised herself as a man. Dr. Barry graduated and became an outstanding doctor. She was the first woman doctor in Canada and acted as Inspector-General of Hospitals. She spent her entire life disguised as a man. Not until her death in 1865, at the age of 71, was her secret discovered.

■ Young girls worked for 60 hours a week for 80 cents, or less than 2 cents an hour.

LIMITED CHOICES

This is the situation women faced at the beginning of the twentieth century:

1. No woman had the right to vote. The Election Act of the Dominion of Canada stated: "no woman, idiot, lunatic, or criminal shall vote."
2. No woman could be elected to federal or provincial offices in government.
3. The father had complete control over his children. He could collect his children's income and even put his children up for adoption without consulting the mother.
4. It was commonly accepted that a woman's chief function was to perform housework for her husband and bear his children. One out of every five women in Canada died in childbirth during this time.
5. Wives had to obey their husbands and could legally be beaten.
6. In the West, wives or single women could not claim homesteads. Only if she was the head of a household could a woman take up a homestead.
7. Married women had the right to financial support from their husbands. However, in practice, wives and children of alcoholic men found it very difficult to collect any support money.
8. Girls could attend elementary and secondary schools, but very few women in Canada went on to gain a post-secondary school education.

■ The National Council of Women was founded in the late 1800s. These women actively sought to achieve social reform, better education for women, and women's right to vote.

Women Find a VOICE

Throughout the nineteenth century, women established a variety of organizations designed to treat social problems. They were concerned about alcoholism, dangerous factory conditions, slum conditions in the cities, impure water and milk, and child abuse.

By the 1880s, many middle-class women began to believe that society would be more moral if women were allowed to vote. The campaign to get women the vote was called the women's suffrage movement. The movement was fuelled by the gender inequality of wages, and its leaders were women who sympathized with the terrible plight of working women. Well-educated, professional women, such as Dr. Emily Stowe and Nellie McClung, provided the early leadership for the women's suffrage movement.

Nellie McClung

Nellie McClung was born in Ontario on October 20, 1873. She was the youngest child in a family of six children. McClung became a teacher, novelist, lecturer, politician, historian, and **prohibitionist**. She raised five children, campaigned for women's suffrage, and sat as a member of the Alberta Legislature. She also wrote sixteen successful books. Her first book, *Sowing Seeds in Danny*, was a humorous look at small-town family life. It sold more than 100,000 copies.

■ Nellie McClung lived in Winnipeg from 1911 1915. There, she became a speaker for the wom rights and reform movement. McClung was kno for her speaking style, which combined comedy and persuasion.

FURTHER UNDERSTANDING

Dr. Emily Stowe Born in Norwich, Ontario, Stowe worked as a teacher before becoming the first licensed Canadian woman doctor. She received her medical training in the United States because no Canadian medical school would accept female students. In 1876, she and her friends formed Canada's first women's suffrage society.

Suffrage The right to vote, or "suffrage," is also known as "the franchise." For many years, only a few wealthy men were allowed to vote. A very small number of people had the power to make decisions for the entire population. Gradually, as people's ideas changed, other groups of people were given the franchise. Men no longer required great wealth and property in order to have the right to vote. Women finally won the same voting rights as men. Women's federal and provincial right to vote was obtained from 1916 to 1925. The only exception was Quebec, where women did not receive the right to vote in provincial elections until 1940. As time passed, the Canadian system of government has become more and more democratic.

While McClung made valuable contributions in many areas, she is best known for her role as a leader in the fight for women's social and political rights. She demanded that women be treated as political equals to men. She once declared: "We are not here to ask for a reform or a gift or a favor, but for a right—not for mercy but for justice. Have we not the brains to think, the hands to work, hearts to feel, and lives to live? Do we not bear our part in citizenship? Do we not help to build the empire?" She was convinced of women's value in society, and she never ceased to fight for their right to be true citizens by being given the right to vote.

On January 27, 1914, Nellie McClung and other suffragists staged a mock parliament to ridicule the Manitoba government for its refusal to grant the franchise to women. In this mock parliament, roles were reversed and men pleaded for the right to vote. Nellie played the premier of the province and responded: "We wish to compliment this delegation on their splendid gentlemanly appearance. If, without exercising the vote, such splendid specimens of manhood can be produced, such a system of affairs should not be interfered with. Any system of civilization that can produce such splendid specimens … is good enough for me, and if it is good enough for me it is good enough for anybody. Another trouble is that if men start to vote they will vote too much. Politics unsettles men, and unsettled men mean unsettled bills—broken furniture, broken vows, and divorce."

The play was a tremendous success. It created uproarious laughter among the audience, great embarrassment for the premier, and many requests to repeat the performance.

The Right to Vote

On January 1, 1919, all Canadian women obtained the federal franchise. They had struggled for nearly 50 years for their right to a voice in government. Winning the franchise did not immediately solve all of the inequalities women faced. It did, however, give women power to begin effecting change. Their voice could now be represented in government.

■ On March 4, 1981, the Canadian Feminists stamp collection was launched. Each woman featured made a significant contribution to women's rights.

The Klondike GOLD RUSH

As word of their discovery spread, thousands of miners and tradespeople came from around the world.

In 1896, Canadian prospectors George Washington Carmack and his brothers-in-law Skokum Jim and Tagish Charlie found a rich deposit of gold on Rabbit Creek, in the Klondike River valley in the Yukon, near present-day Dawson City.

When several miners took a steamship from Alaska to the West Coast the following July, their loads of gold caused great excitement. As word of their discovery spread, thousands of miners and tradespeople came from around the world.

Many gold seekers did not realize the difficulties and delays they would face. Different routes could be taken. Those who could afford it, travelled all the way on water. Others journeyed over the Chilkoot Pass or the White Pass. When winter came, many could not make it through the White Pass. More than 25,000 people travelled the Chilkoot Pass, carrying heavy loads on their backs and on sleds to the summit. Sometimes, two or three trips were required to transport all of the necessary supplies. People would then have to travel the Yukon River by boat. Some spent as long as two years on the trail. Regardless of the route, it was a slow and challenging trip.

Dawson City became Canada's biggest city west of Winnipeg. The North-West Mounted Police set up a post in the Chilkoot Pass where they collected **duty**. They were kept busy preventing poorly equipped gold seekers from venturing into the wilderness—anyone without enough supplies to last a year was turned back. In addition, they maintained order among the rough prospectors. They would not hesitate to take away firearms or to send criminals out of the Yukon. A special military unit, the Yukon Field Force, ensured that the region remained Canadian territory despite the arrival of numerous Americans.

FURTHER UNDERSTANDING

George W. Carmack George W. Carmack had been working on the Chilkoot Pass as a **packer**. He also prospected for gold. Another prospector, Robert Henderson, told him about possible gold deposits in the area. It was a great tip. The creek was so plentiful with gold it was later named Bonanza Creek. Carmack and his brothers-in-law staked their claims. The claims were recorded at Forty Mile, a mining camp, and Carmack and his relatives became very rich.

Chilkoot Pass Like the White Pass, this Pass is located on the British Columbia–Alaska border. The Tlingit originally used the pass as a trading route. It was also used by Americans when they came to study the area in the 1880s. It is estimated that between 20,000 and 30,000 people crossed the pass during the Gold Rush.

Dawson City Located where the Yukon and Klondike Rivers meet, Dawson City was originally an Aboriginal fishing camp. By the peak of the Gold Rush, in the late 1800s, Dawson City had a population of about 20,000. It was surrounded by prospectors staking claims on nearby hills and rivers. Saloons, gambling parlours, dance halls, theatres, and stores met the needs of the new population.

■ Barkerville was established in 1862 during the first British Columbian Gold Rush along the Fraser River. Within one year, the population of Barkerville had grown to 10,000 people. After the Gold Rush years, Barkerville became little more than a ghost town.

TREATIES IN THE NORTH

The government had been eager to sign treaties with the Aboriginal peoples on the plains in the 1870s and 1880s to smooth the way for settlement. Since the north was not useful for farming, the government did not negotiate with the Aboriginal peoples there. In the 1890s, Chief Kinosayoo of the Woodland Cree began requesting treaty negotiations.

He wanted help for his people to make the transition to a different way of life. He also wanted to protect their rights among non-Aboriginal trappers and settlers. The Cree wanted to continue hunting, fishing, and trapping while getting assistance for farming, education, and medical needs.

Negotiations finally began when prospectors started travelling through Aboriginal lands to the Yukon. Some of the prospectors caused trouble, shooting dogs and destroying traps. The government negotiated Treaty Eight in 1899 in order to prevent bloodshed. Other treaties followed as northern resources were discovered and developed.

RESULTS of the Rush

Many miners spent their money as fast as they made it.

The Yukon Territory was populated by about 35,000 people during the Gold Rush. The Gold Rush, however, was short-lived and ended almost as quickly as it had begun. News of gold in Alaska caused many to leave almost overnight. The surface gold deposits of the area were depleted. By 1899, only a few people remained in Dawson City. Today, just over 1,000 people live there.

In the end, few prospectors actually got rich. Before many arrived, the best claims had been staked. About $50 million in gold came out of the Yukon. Many miners spent their money as fast as they made it, and some never managed to make back the money it cost them to get there. However, the Gold Rush had enabled some of the Aboriginal peoples in the North to get the treaties they wanted. Furthermore, the Canadian government was prompted to settle boundary issues with the United States and establish territorial control.

The Alaska Dispute

After Confederation, all dealings between Canada and other countries were still handled by Great Britain. This caused a problem when the United States and Canada disagreed about the ownership of the Pacific Coast.

Although the United States had purchased Alaska from Russia in 1867, the boundaries between Canada and Alaska were not set. As a result of the Gold Rush in 1898, access to the Yukon from Pacific ports became important. Both Canada and the United States claimed ownership. In 1903, a panel of three Americans, two Canadians, and one British judge considered the matter. The British judge sided with the Americans. Canadians were bitter. The country had learned it was important for Canada to be independent as a nation.

■ An international panel was assigned to solve the Alaska boundary dispute. The p[a] sided with the Americans. While the settlement promoted anti-British feelings in Can[a] it did build better relations between Britain and the United States.

Yukon Territory

Tens of thousands of people had flooded to the Yukon prompted by the Gold Rush. In an effort to control the area, the government officially separated it from the North-West Territories in 1898. The federal government appointed a commissioner, James Walsh, to govern the Yukon Territory. A five-member Council was also appointed. The first capital city was Dawson City. Elected officials were eventually added, beginning with two members in 1900.

ROBERT W. SERVICE

Robert W. Service was born in England in 1874 and came to Canada in 1896. He worked for the Canadian Bank of Commerce in British Columbia, which sent him to the Yukon in 1904. Even though he arrived there after the Gold Rush, he wrote several poems about it and eventually published *Songs of a Sourdough*. He also wrote a novel, *The Trail of '98,* while living in Dawson, ten years after the rush. One of his most popular poems is "The Cremation of Sam McGee."

Excerpts from "The Cremation of Sam McGee"

There are strange things done in the midnight sun
By the men who moil for gold;
The Arctic trails have their secret tales
That would make your blood run cold;
The Northern Lights have seen queer sights,
But the queerest they ever did see
Was that night on the marge of Lake Lebarge
I cremated Sam McGee …
 … On a Christmas Day we were mushing our way
over the Dawson trail.
Talk of your cold! Through the parka's fold
It stabbed like a driven nail.
If our eyes we'd close, then the lashes froze
till sometimes we couldn't see,
It wasn't much fun, but the only one
to whimper was Sam McGee …

■ Robert W. Service wrote many of his poems and stories while he was living in a small cabin in Dawson.

Sir Wilfrid LAURIER

As the nineteenth century drew to a close and the twentieth century began, Canada entered a period of great prosperity. This was also a time of cultural conflict and change. Sir Wilfrid Laurier, a Liberal Roman Catholic lawyer from Québec, held the reins of Canadian government during this challenging time.

Laurier became prime minister in 1896. For the next fifteen years, he tried to solve the problems caused by Canada's relationship with both Britain and the United States. He sought to steer a course of compromise between the British imperialists and the French nationalists. Above all, Laurier was a strong promoter of national unity. He believed in Canada's future as a strong, independent nation. At Colonial Conferences in 1897 and 1902,

he firmly resisted Britain's efforts to unify the British Empire. Canada could stand on its own.

Laurier's policy of compromise was not always successful. Many French Canadians were outraged in 1899 when he agreed to pay some of the costs of transporting and equipping Canadians wishing to fight for Britain in the Boer War. Laurier angered French Canadians again in 1905 when he did not protect Catholic education rights in Saskatchewan and Alberta. He bowed to the pressure of the English Protestant

FURTHER UNDERSTANDING

Imperialists Canadian imperialists wanted Canada to play a greater role in matters of the British Empire. They wanted to establish closer economic, political, cultural, and military relations with Britain. Imperialists believed that as Canada's population grew, it would soon play a major role in the British Empire.

Nationalists Nationalists believed in a nation independent of British control. They believed in a strong Canadian government that made its own decisions on foreign and economic policy. Some French nationalists rejected outright any British influence at all. Instead, they wished to emphasize, preserve, and promote their French-Canadian culture. Others, such as Henri

Bourassa, grandson of Louis-Joseph Papineau, wanted a bilingual and bicultural country.

Reciprocity Agreement A system of free trade involves the exchange of goods between countries. Trade is permitted without taxes, duties, or certain restrictions imposed by government. The Reciprocity Agreement outlined the free trade of several natural products from farms, forests, and fisheries. It also reduced duty on many Canadian manufactured products entering the United States. Many Canadians were not ready to accept free trade with the United States. They were afraid of being both economically and politically swallowed by their powerful neighbour.

■ The first Canadian Pacific Railway locomotive reached Vancouver in 1884. Sir Wilfred Laurier planned to build a second transcontinental line in 1903.

majority and did not provide a separate Catholic school system in the new western provinces.

In an effort to promote Canadian unity, Laurier revealed plans to construct a second transcontinental railway in 1903. It would consist of two lines: the government-funded National Transcontinental between Moncton and Winnipeg, and the Grand Trunk Pacific line from Winnipeg westward. He also allowed a third transcontinental railway to be built by the Canadian Northern Railway. This eventually put a large financial burden on the country since much of the railway building was at public expense.

Divided Loyalties

Laurier was returned to office in the 1900, 1904, and 1908 elections. In 1910, he introduced the Naval Service Bill to create a Canadian navy. The five cruisers and six destroyers in the navy would fight alongside Britain as needed. Once again,

many French Canadians were angered by this measure. Many English Canadians were not satisfied either. They thought Laurier should have donated the money for these ships to Britain. Laurier was finally defeated in 1911, in part because the French-Canadian nationalists thought his government was too British and the English imperialists thought it was not British enough. Laurier's compromises had pleased no one.

The other major reason for Laurier's defeat in 1911 was his proposed Reciprocity Agreement with the United States. Laurier was firm in his belief that the trade agreement would help Canada prosper and grow as a nation. Canadians did not agree and his government was defeated by the Conservatives in 1911.

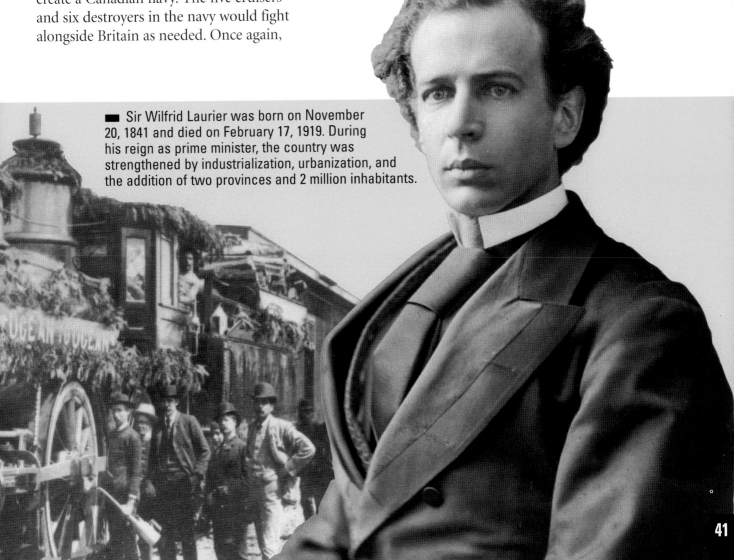

■ Sir Wilfrid Laurier was born on November 20, 1841 and died on February 17, 1919. During his reign as prime minister, the country was strengthened by industrialization, urbanization, and the addition of two provinces and 2 million inhabitants.

The Boer WAR

During the course of the war, many Canadians distinguished themselves for bravery.

In 1899, Britain went to war with the **Afrikaner** republics in South Africa. Britain wanted to keep its place as the head of a powerful, united empire. However, the Afrikaners were willing to fight for their independence and their homeland.

British Canadians put pressure on the government to aid Britain by sending troops to the African battlefields. However, many French Canadians felt Canada should play no part in this conflict. They did not want their children dying in a far-away war to help Britain maintain its empire. Their sympathies laid more with the Afrikaners.

Prime Minister Laurier tried to compromise. He sent a small group of 1,000 troops as well as nurses and blacksmiths. This was the first significant body of Canadian soldiers to serve overseas. Canada paid part of the costs of recruiting, clothing, equipping, and transporting the troops. Britain and a few private individuals covered the rest of the cost, and also sent more troops later as the war dragged on.

Britain made many mistakes and suffered many defeats in the early part of the war. The war turned into dirty, drawn-out guerrilla warfare. Eventually, Britain was able to win with new leadership and more reinforcements.

During the course of the war, many Canadians distinguished themselves for bravery, winning several medals and awards. Four Canadians received the Victoria Cross, 19 received the Distinguished Service Order, 17 more were awarded Distinguished Conduct medals, and 117 were mentioned in dispatches for bravery. Canada's senior nursing sister was awarded the Royal Red Cross.

While there was a sense of pride, Canada was divided with regards to its involvement in the war. The war increased tensions between French and British Canadians. Some British Canadians felt that Laurier had not done enough to help Great Britain. Many French Canadians, however, believed that Canada should not have become involved at all.

■ Several thousand Canadian volunteers took part in the Boer War.

FURTHER UNDERSTANDING

Victoria Cross In 1856, Queen Victoria created the highest award for bravery in battle—the Victoria Cross. She wished to acknowledge exceptional bravery in the **Crimean War**. The medals were crafted from Russian cannons taken by the British during the war. Since then, many medals have been awarded to Commonwealth citizens for valour. When other bravery awards came into being, the Victoria Cross was discontinued. However, at the request of the Canadian government, Queen Elizabeth II approved a Canadian Victoria Cross award.

ALBERTA and Saskatchewan

During Laurier's four terms in office, the population grew rapidly in the North-West Territories. Soon, the people living there began to demand provincial status. At this time, the North-West Territories was in a similar political position to Upper and Lower Canada in the 1830s. The region was, in many ways, a colony of the federal government. It was granted representative government in 1888 and responsible government in 1897.

In 1905, Prime Minister Wilfrid Laurier finally bowed to public pressure. First, he had to decide how many provinces to create and where the boundaries would be. Territorial premier Frederick Haultain wanted one large province. Manitoba premier Rodmond Roblin suggested that his province be enlarged westward to create two evenly-sized provinces. The people who argued for two new provinces could not agree whether the provinces should be divided along north and south or east and west lines.

Laurier eventually chose the 60th parallel as the northern boundary because cereal grains could not grow north of this line. The east–west division along 110° longitude created two equal-sized provinces, Alberta and Saskatchewan, in 1905. In 1912, Manitoba, Ontario, and Québec were extended to their current size.

Alberta and Saskatchewan were not granted control of their natural resources and **crown lands**. However, they would have publicly funded province-wide school systems, with allowances for denominational schools if numbers warranted. In addition, they would have the financial support of the federal government, for such things as the development of public works.

> **Laurier eventually chose the 60th parallel as the northern boundary because cereal grains could not grow north of this line.**

How the Provinces Evolved from 1867–1949

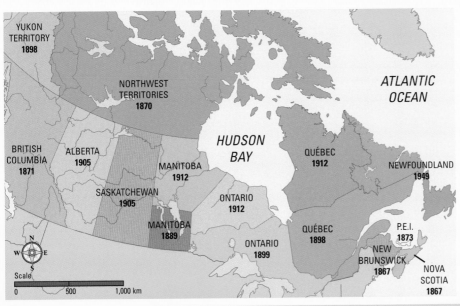

YUKON TERRITORY 1898

NORTHWEST TERRITORIES 1870

ATLANTIC OCEAN

HUDSON BAY

BRITISH COLUMBIA 1871

ALBERTA 1905

MANITOBA 1912

QUÉBEC 1912

NEWFOUNDLAND 1949

SASKATCHEWAN 1905

ONTARIO 1912

MANITOBA 1889

QUÉBEC 1898

P.E.I. 1873

ONTARIO 1899

NEW BRUNSWICK 1867

NOVA SCOTIA 1867

N W E S

Scale
0   500   1,000 km

FURTHER UNDERSTANDING

Denominational school system In a denominational school system, education is tied to a particular religious group. For example, the Manitoba Act allowed publicly funded Catholic schools.

Public school system A publicly funded school system is one that is supported by tax dollars. In this system, all children have access to an education.

Multiple Choice

Choose the best answer in the multiple choice questions that follow:

1 Which of the following was not part of Sir John A. Macdonald's National Policy?
a) protective tariffs
b) Aboriginal treaties
c) settlement of the West
d) a transcontinental railway

2 What was the reason for Macdonald's resignation in 1873?
a) the North-West Rebellion
b) the Red River Resistance
c) the Reciprocity Agreement
d) the Pacific Scandal

3 Which of the following was not a term of the Numbered Treaties?
a) Aboriginal peoples would receive money each year
b) the Canadian government would provide the Aboriginal peoples with farm animals and equipment
c) Aboriginal lands would be returned after 100 years
d) Aboriginal peoples would have access to medicine and government assistance in the event of an epidemic

4 When did Canadian women obtain the right to vote?
a) December 12, 1878
b) January 27, 1914
c) January 1, 1919
d) March 6, 1923

5 What was Sir Wilfrid Laurier's compromise during the Boer War?
a) Canada would split the cost with Britain of sending a small group of troops
b) Canada would only supply support people, such as nurses
c) Canada would help finance the war, but would not send troops
d) both b) and c)

6 Which of the following was not a result of the Klondike Gold Rush?
a) the creation of a border between Alaska and the Yukon
b) the establishment of treaties with northern Aboriginal groups
c) the creation of the Yukon Territory
d) the establishment of a wealthy middle-class in Dawson City

7 Who said, "We are not here to ask for a reform or a gift or a favor, but for a right—not for mercy but for justice"?
a) Sir Wilfrid Laurier
b) Sir John A. Macdonald
c) Chief Big Bear
d) Nellie McClung

Mix and Match

Match the terms in column B with the correct description in column A. There are more terms than descriptions.

A

1. Prime minister of Canada between 1873 and 1878
2. Signed a treaty in 1882 to prevent starvation
3. Launched an advertising campaign to promote settlement of the West
4. Arrested Louis Riel
5. First discovered gold in the Klondike River Valley
6. Supported the idea of compulsory, free, and universal education
7. First licensed Canadian woman doctor

B

a) Chief Big Bear
b) Egerton Ryerson
c) Emily Stowe
d) George W. Carmack
e) Sam Steele
f) Alexander Mackenzie
g) James Walsh
h) Clifford Sifton
i) Nellie McClung

Time Line

Find the appropriate spot on the time line for each event listed below:

A Macdonald is re-elected

B The Battle of Batoche ends the North-West Rebellion

C Construction begins on the transcontinental railway

D Alberta and Saskatchewan are created

E The North-West Mounted Police is created

F Beginning of the Boer War

July 1, 1867 The Province of Canada, New Brunswick, and Nova Scotia unite to form the Dominion of Canada

1870 The province of Manitoba is created

1871 British Columbia enters Confederation

1873 Prince Edward Island enters Confederation

1873 **1**
1873 John A. Macdonald resigns

1878 **2**
1874 The NWMP begin its Great March West

1875 **3**
1885 The last spike of the transcontinental railway is pounded in Eagle Pass

1885 **4**
1896 Gold is discovered in the Klondike River Valley

1898 Yukon Territory is created

1899 **5**

1905 **6**

Conclusion

In 1873, the Pacific Scandal delayed railway plans and resulted in the resignation of John A. Macdonald. Mackenzie's Liberal government worked half-heartedly on the railway until Macdonald regained power in 1878.

Violence on the lawless Prairies prompted the creation of the North-West Mounted Police. The NWMP helped patrol Canada's western frontier and put an end to the North-West Rebellion in the mid-1880s. The rebellion was caused by Métis land-rights concerns. The Métis were eventually defeated at Batoche.

By 1885, the great transcontinental railway, built by the Canadian Pacific Railway, was complete. The West was open to settlement.

In 1896, Wilfrid Laurier became prime minister during the Gold Rush period in the north. The Gold Rush resulted in the creation of a new territory—the Yukon. In 1899, the Boer War divided the country when Laurier sent troops to Africa. Later, in 1905, Laurier created two new provinces—Alberta and Saskatchewan. Laurier's proposed Reciprocity Agreement with the United States lost him the next election.

The late 1800s and early 1900s were a period of great change in Canada. Industries and labour unions sprung up across the country. New laws were created to protect children, and women obtained the federal franchise in 1919. Canada emerged from this period of growth and conflict as a nation. Work was still needed, especially in the development of national unity, but the path was set and the journey had begun.

Further Information

Suggested Reading

Berton, Pierre. *Klondike: The Last Great Gold Rush, 1896–1899.* Toronto: Doubleday Canada, 2001.

Brown, Wayne F. *Steele's Scouts: Samuel Benfield Steele and the North-West Rebellion.* Nanoose Bay, B.C.: Heritage House, 2001.

Creighton, Donald G. *John A. Macdonald: The Young Politician and the Old Chieftain.* Toronto: University of Toronto Press, 1998.

LaPierre, Laurier. *Sir Wilfrid Laurier & the Romance of Canada.* Toronto: Stoddart Publishing, 1996.

Internet Resources

Canada: A People's History Online
history.cbc.ca
The online companion to CBC's award-winning television series on the history of Canada, as told through the eyes of its people. This multi-media Web site features behind-the-scenes information, games and puzzles, and discussion boards. Available in French and English.

The Canadian Encyclopedia Online
www.thecanadianencyclopedia.com
A fantastic reference for all things Canadian. Excellent history articles are accompanied by photographs, paintings, and maps. Articles can be read in both French and English.

Glossary

absentee landlords: those who own land but do not live on it

Afrikaner: inhabitant of South Africa who is of Dutch descent

bloomers: loose shorts gathered at the knee; once worn by women when playing sports

British Empire: Great Britain and all the territories under its control

charter: a grant from a government or company permitting the formation of an organization with certain privileges

Conservative: belonging to the Conservative Party, which favours traditional views and values

Crimean War: a war in Crimea between Russia and a group of nations including Britain, France, and Turkey; lasted from 1853 to 1856

crown lands: public land that belongs to the government

duty: a government tax, especially on goods taken into or out of a country

guerrilla warfare: type of warfare that relies on sudden raids and ambushes

Liberal: belonging to the Liberal Party, which favours progress and reform

Métis: a person descended from both Aboriginal peoples and Europeans

packer: someone who transports goods to remote places

persecution: treated badly, often for political, racial, or religious reasons

prohibitionist: someone who supports laws that prohibit the manufacture and sale of alcohol

responsible government: in Canada, a government that is responsible to the representatives of the people

Standard Time: the official time used in any given region; the world is divided into twenty-four standard time zones

treaty: a signed agreement between two or more nations

voyageur: a boatperson, usually a French Canadian, in the service of early fur-trading companies

Answers

Multiple Choice	Mix and Match	Time Line
1. b)	1. f)	1. e)
2. d)	2. a)	2. a)
3. c)	3. h)	3. c)
4. c)	4. e)	4. b)
5. a)	5. d)	5. f)
6. d)	6. a)	6. d)
7. d)	7. c)	

Index